Who Goes There?

Who goes there, in the night,
   Across the storm-swept plain?
We are the ghosts of a valiant war —
   A million murdered men!

Who goes there, at the dawn,
   Across the sun-swept plain?
We are the hosts of those who swear:
   It shall not be again!

                       Thomas Curtis Clark

ONE HUNDRED POEMS OF PEACE

AN ANTHOLOGY

COMPILED BY
THOMAS CURTIS CLARK
AND
WINFRED ERNEST GARRISON

Granger Index Reprint Series

Originally published by
WILLETT, CLARK & COMPANY
Chicago, New York

BOOKS FOR LIBRARIES PRESS
FREEPORT, NEW YORK

Copyright 1934 by Willett, Clark & Company

Copyright renewed 1962 by Mrs. Hazel P. Davis Clark

All rights reserved

Reprinted 1971 by arrangement with
Harper & Row, Publishers, Inc.

INTERNATIONAL STANDARD BOOK NUMBER:
0-8369-6265-6

LIBRARY OF CONGRESS CATALOG CARD NUMBER:
75-160902

PRINTED IN THE UNITED STATES OF AMERICA
BY
NEW WORLD BOOK MANUFACTURING CO., INC.
HALLANDALE, FLORIDA 33009

FOREWORD

As a theme for verse, war has been second only to love. It is curious that these two topics which cancel each other out should have engaged the attention of the poets to so large a degree. Yet not so strange after all, for both are the expressions of intense and colorful passions. Peace has seemed but a pallid and demure (and not very interesting) virgin in comparison with Venus and the Valkyries.

Yet there has been a poetry of peace, and its low, insistent note refuses to be drowned out by trumpet and drum. Peace is becoming an affirmative thing, not the empty interval between wars. It is awakening a passion no less intense and vivid than the truculence of war or the fierce possessiveness of love. It can be sung as well as preached, and it cannot be well preached or wisely negotiated unless it is sung.

Here are a hundred (and more) poems of peace, some old, some new. Many of them are not easily accessible in other books. All of them are valid expressions of the great fact of human brotherhood and of the heart's hunger for friendliness and reason and justice, without which no art can long survive.

ONE HUNDRED
POEMS OF PEACE

The Desire of Nations

And the government shall be upon his shoulder: and his name shall be called Wonderful, Counsellor, the Mighty God, The Everlasting Father, The Prince of Peace. — Isaiah.

Earth will go back to her lost youth,
And life grow deep and wonderful as truth,
When the wise King out of the nearing Heaven comes
To break the spell of long millenniums —
To build with song again
The broken hopes of men —
To hush and heroize the world,
Under the flag of Brotherhood unfurled.
And He will come some day:
Already is His star upon the way!
He comes, O world, He comes!
But not with bugle-cry nor roll of doubling drums.

Nay, for He comes to loosen and unbind,
To build the lofty purpose in the mind,
To stir the heart's deep chord. . . .
No rude horns parleying, no shock of shields;
Nor as of old the glory of the Lord
To half-awakened shepherds in the fields,
Looking with foolish faces on the rush
Of the Great Splendor, when the pulsing hush
Came o'er the hills, came o'er the heavens afar
Where on their cliff of stars the watching seraphs are.

Nor as of old when first the Strong One trod,
The Power of sepulchers — our Risen God!
When on that deathless morning in the dark,
He quit the Garden of the Sepulcher,
Setting the oleander boughs astir,
And pausing at the gate with backward hark.
Nay, nor as when the Hero-King of Heaven
Came with upbraiding to his faint Eleven,
And found the world-way to his bright feet barred,
And hopeless then because men's hearts were hard.

Nor will He come like carnal kings of old,
With pomp of pilfered gold;
Nor like the pharisees with pride of prayer;
Nor as the stumbling foolish stewards dream
In tedious argument and milkless creed.
But in the passion of the heart-warm deed
Will come the Man Supreme.
Yea, for He comes to lift the Public Care —
To build on earth the Vision hung in air.

This is the one fulfillment of his Law —
The one Fact in the mockeries that seem.
This is the vision that the prophets saw —
The Comrade Kingdom builded in their dream.
   No, not as in that elder day
Comes now the King upon the human way.
He comes with power: his white unfearing face
Shines through the Social Passion of the race.
He comes to frame the freedom of the Law,
To touch these men of earth
With a feeling of life's oneness and its worth,
A feeling of its mystery and awe.

And when He comes into the world gone wrong.
He will rebuild her beauty with a song.
To every heart He will its own dream be:
One moon has many phantoms in the sea.
Out of the North the horns will cry to men:
' Baldur the Beautiful has come again! '
The flutes of Greece will whisper from the dead:
' Apollo has unveiled his sunbright head! '
The stones of Thebes and Memphis will find voice:
' Osiris comes: O tribes of Time, rejoice! '
And social architects who build the State,
Serving the Dream at citadel and gate,
Will hail Him coming through the labor-hum.
And glad quick cries will go from man to man:
' Lo, He has come, our Christ the Artisan —
The King who loved the lilies, He has come! '

He will arrive, our Counselor and Chief;
And with bleak faces lighted up will come
The earth-worn mothers from their martyrdom,
To tell Him of their grief.
And glad girls caroling from field and town
Will go to meet Him with the labor-crown,
The new crown woven of the heading wheat.
And men will sit down at his sacred feet;
And He will say — the King —
' Come, let us live the poetry we sing! '
And these, his burning words, will break the ban —
Words that will grow to be
On continent, on sea,
The rallying cry of man. . . .
He comes to make the long injustice right —
Comes to push back the shadow of the night,
The gray Tradition full of flint and flaw —

Comes to wipe out the insults to the soul,
The insults of the Few against the Whole,
The insults they make righteous with a law.

Yea, He will bear the Safety of the State;
For in his still and rhythmic steps will be
The power and music of Alcyone,
Who holds the swift heavens in their starry fate.
Yea, He will lay on souls the power of peace,
And send on kingdoms torn the sense of home —
More than the fire of Joy that burned on Greece,
More than the light of Law that rose on Rome.
Edwin Markham

Dawn

The hour of dawn is the hour of death —
I know by the gas in the morning's breath;
I know by the cannon's racking scream,
By the rifle's click, by the bayonet's gleam;
I know by our crouching, hushed platoon
That the word is near, that the hour is soon
When we'll leap to the top with the shibboleth —
'*The hour of dawn is the hour of death!*'

The hour of dawn is the hour of life!
A new world springs from a world of strife!
A world uncursed by autocracy's brood;
A world of beauty and brotherhood;
A world made true to a holy plan —
The reign of love, the rule of Man!
It is hate and lust and war we knife —
The hour of dawn is the hour of life!

Daniel Henderson

Victory Without Peace

The slaughter-bugles screamed once more,
   Over the patchwork lands of men,
And scattered, sword-hewn empires tore
   Each other's greedy hearts again —

One with a black and boastful greed,
   Seeking a red supremacy;
The other with a mumbled creed
   That it was armed to make men free.

Each steppe and pampa woke to flame
   And joined the berserker advance;
From wild forgotten roads they came,
   For the world's roads all led to France.

And now no more the hail of steel
   Tortures the lines of brown and gray. . . .
The brief, joy-mad processions reel
   And drop . . . and it is peace, men say.

Peace? When wherever men are found
   The victors cry, ' But just so free! '
And reddened banners spring from the ground
   For freer red supremacy. . . .

A hollow shell of victory,
   With war still writhing at its heart;
A clipped and gelded liberty,
   Striving to force its chains apart!

Yet solvent love is not too far,
   If men grow wise, or mobs stay kind;
And we could calm this troubled star,
   Its singing rapture unconfined.

Now take your choice, O you who hoard
   Frail-fingered power, weak lordly breath:
Young freedom, or the age-scarred sword
   Which leaves no peace on earth — but death.
Clement Wood

Gold Stars

Gold stars looking on the far French crosses,
   Trembling softly in the unscarred sky,
Flash to us the meaning of our dear, deep losses,
   Show us how to steer to the Hope that made men die!
Golden lives of youth, they were given without measure;
   Hear we not the question, flung to you and me,
' What have you bought with us, your golden treasure,
   You that sent us over sea? '

Gold stars worn upon the hearts of mothers,
   Sad, starry flowers from the furrows of war,
Bear to us the message of the sons and brothers
   Fallen in the far fields, absent evermore:
' What did you spend us for, your golden treasure?
   Hate and pride and vengeance? Then you paid too high!
Or was it for a World that you poured us without measure?
   That was what we meant to buy! '

Gold stars gleaming on the flags' red borders
   In the sacred places where our altars are,
Speak to us your oracles, shout to us your orders,
   Bid us climb to brotherhood, following a Star:
' You must buy a World with us, your golden treasure;
   You must buy a new World, else you hold us cheap!
So shall we rejoice that you poured us without measure,
   So shall we rejoice in our sleep.'
Helen Gray Cone

Peace on Earth

The men of the earth said: 'We must war
   As the men of the earth have warred;
'Tis ours to wield on the battlefield
   The unrelenting sword.'
But they who had seen the valiant die,
The fathers of men, they answered 'Why?'

The men of the earth said: 'We must arm,
   For so we would reveal
The nobler part of the human heart,
   The love of the nation's weal.'
But they who had sung their lullaby,
The mothers of men, they answered, 'Why?'

The men of the earth said: 'We must fight,
   For so the fit survive;
By the jungle law of fang and claw
   The strong are kept alive.'
But a crippled, cankered progeny,
The sons of the fighters, answered, 'Why?'

The men of the earth said: 'We must fall,
   And falling build the road
O'er which the race with quickening pace
   Can find its way to God.'
But down from a Cross uplifted high,
The Savior of men, He answered, 'Why?'
                              Robert Freeman

Cry of the Dead

Silence the hateful mortar's lying mutter;
   Silence the drums loud perjury; the quick
Falsehood of bullets; the machine-gun's stutter;
   And all the bellowing cannon's rhetoric!

Silence them all: the rifle's rapid lies;
   Silence the bugle's treacherous evasion;
Silence the shrapnel's shrill and ghoulish cries;
   The bayonet's abrupt and false persuasion!

Out of the forum of our hush, we dead
   Cry out above the cannon and the drum:
Never from any slaying, any dread
   Will spring to flower the millennium!

Begin rebuilding Eden once more: start
   Healing all broken, parted peoples whole:
There is no other nation but the heart;
   There is no other country but the soul!

Louis Ginsberg

The Hymn of Hate

And this I hate — not men, nor flag, nor race,
But only War with its wild, grinning face.
God strike it till its eyes be blind as night
And all its members tremble with affright!
Oh, let it hear in its death agony
The wail of mothers for their best-loved ones,
      And on its head
Descend the venomed curses of its sons
Who followed her, deluded, where its guns
      Had dyed the daisies red.

All these I hate — war and its panoply,
The lie that hides its ghastly mockery,
That makes its glories out of women's tears,
The toil of peasants through the burdened years,
The legacy of long disease that preys
On bone and body in the after-days.
   God's curses pour,
Until it shrivel with its votaries
And die away in its own fiery seas,
   That nevermore
Its dreadful call of murder may be heard;
A thing accursed in very deed and word
    From blood-drenched shore to shore!
Joseph Dana Miller

Elegy for Mars

Upon our highest hill, within a clod
Appropriately consecrated, lies
The hero of all holocaust. Now rise
Tumultuous entreaties to a god
Who has forsaken us, whose holy rod
Must nevermore be raised to blind our eyes:
The march of armies and their battlecries
Are buried under furrows of turned sod.

His drums are broken, his frayed banners furled,
His corps disbanded and his bugles mute,
When we who are the liberated world
Can plough and plant and harvest golden fruit
In peaceful orchards, who dared not before
We heaped our stones upon the grave of war.
Carl John Bostelmann

Wild Weather

A great wind sweeps
Across the world, hurling to heaps
Of gilded rubbish crowns and thrones, mere gleam
And flicker of dry leaves in its fierce path,
A wind whose very wrath
Springs from white Alpine crests of thought and dream.

What sword can quell
An unleashed tempest, and compel
Hush to the thunder, patience to the storm?
The maddened blast that buffets sea and land
Blows under high command,
Rending and riving only to transform.

May its wild wings
Burst the old tanglement of things,
Those withered vines and brambles that enmesh
The leaping foot! May its rough flail destroy
Hedges that limit joy,
Leaving, like rain, a silvery earth and fresh!

Faith shall not quail
For broken branches of the gale.
Time is a strong corrival and will win.
When hurricane has done its dread behest,
And forests are at rest,
His quiet hand will lead the sunshine in.

Katharine Lee Bates

1914 — and After

Would you end war?
Create great Peace. . . .
The Peace that demands all of a man,
His love, his life, his veriest self;
Plunge him into the smelting fires of a work that becomes
    his child. . . .

Give him a hard Peace; a Peace of discipline and justice. . . .
Kindle him with vision, invite him to joy and adventure:
Set him to work, not to create *things*
But to create *man:*
Yea, himself.

Go search your heart, America. . . .
Turn from the machine to man,
Build, while there is yet time, a creative Peace. . . .
While there is yet time! . . .
For if you reject great Peace,
As surely as vile living brings disease,
So surely will your selfishness bring war.

James Oppenheim

A Confession of Faith

I believe in God, who is for me spirit, love, the principle of all things.

I believe that God is in me, as I am in Him.

I believe that the true welfare of man consists in fulfilling the will of God.

I believe that from the fulfillment of the will of God there can follow nothing but that which is good for me and for all men.

I believe that the will of God is that every man should love his fellowmen, and should act toward others as he desires that they should act toward him.

I believe that the reason of life is for each of us simply to grow in love.

I believe that this growth in love will contribute more than any other force to establish the Kingdom of God on earth —

To replace a social life in which division, falsehood and violence are all-powerful, with a new order in which humanity, truth and brotherhood will reign.

Leo Tolstoy

From 'My Religion'

The Valley of the Shadow

God, I am traveling out to death's sea,
   I who exulted in sunshine and laughter
Thought not of dying — death is such waste of me;
   Grant me one comfort: Leave not the hereafter
Of mankind to war, as though I had died not —
   I who in battle, my comrade's arm linking,
Shouted and sang — life in my pulses hot
   Throbbing and dancing! Let not my sinking
In dark be for naught, my death a vain thing!
   God, let me know it the end of man's fever!
Make my last breath a bugle call, carrying
   Peace o'er the valleys and cold hills forever!

John Galsworthy

The New Mars

I war against the folly that is War,
   The sacrifice that pity hath not stayed,
The Great Delusion men have perished for,
   The lie that hath the souls of men betrayed.
I war for justice and for human right,
Against the lawless tyranny of Might.

A monstrous cult has held the world too long,
   The worship of a Moloch that hath slain
Remorselessly the young, the brave, the strong,
   Indifferent to the unmeasured pain,
The accumulated horror and despair,
That stricken Earth no longer wills to bear.

My goal is *peace* — not peace at any price,
   While yet ensanguined jaws of Evil yawn
Hungry and pitiless: Nay, peace were vice
   Until the cruel dragon-teeth be drawn,
And the wronged victims of Oppression be
Delivered from its hateful rule, and free!

When comes that hour, resentment laid aside,
   Into a ploughshare will I beat my sword;
The weaker nations' strength shall be my pride,
   Their gladness my exceeding great reward;
And not in vain shall be the tears now shed,
Nor vain the service of the gallant dead.

I war against the folly that is War,
   The futile sacrifice that nought hath stayed,
The Great Delusion men have perished for,
   The lie that hath the souls of men betrayed:
For faith I war, humanity and trust;
For peace on earth — a lasting peace, and just!

Florence Earle Coates

A New Earth

God grant us wisdom in these coming days,
    And eyes unsealed, that we clear visions see
Of that new world that He would have us build,
    To Life's ennoblement and His high ministry.

God give us sense — God-sense of Life's new needs,
    And souls aflame with new-born chivalries —
To cope with those black growths that foul the ways —
    To cleanse our poisoned founts with God-born energies.

To pledge our souls with nobler, loftier life,
    To win the world to His fair sanctities,
To bind the nations in a Pact of Peace,
    And free the Soul of Life for finer loyalties.

Not since Christ died upon His lonely cross
    Has time such prospect held of Life's new birth;
Not since the world of chaos first was born
    Has man so clearly visaged hope of a new earth.

Not of our own might can we hope to rise
    Above the ruts and soilures of the past,
But, with His help who did the first earth build,
    With hearts courageous we may fairer build this last.
John Oxenham

Soldiers

Solid mass and heavy might,
On they march to where the bright
Crimson flowers of battle bloom
And bear the iron fruit of doom.

They are flesh and bone and blood:
They trample very earth to mud:
Earth is shaken with the tread
Of the anticipatory dead.

The laughing flesh goes marching on
Toward the grinning skeleton:
On they tramp, these solid hosts —
Army of the million ghosts!

Merrill Root

Which Sword?

A sword, a sword, and a sword;
  Which sword will you draw, my Son?
For one is of steel with its blind appeal
  Till the folly of war is done.
'Tis an honor to fight for God and the right
  But justice is seldom won.

And one is the sword of truth,
  God's swift and naked blade
That puts to flight the lies of night
  And the hatred falsehoods made.
We are cowards all when lies appall,
  But in truth we are unafraid.

And one is a flaming sword
  Whose work is but begun;
Its glorious part is to change the heart,
  Its victories always won.
Draw this and smite with all thy might —
  'Tis the sword of love, my Son.

Jason Noble Pierce

Ultimatum

We will not fight!
The rolling drum and trumpet call no more
Excite. We were as foolish boys before,
But now we think as men. Our loyalty
To truth, to human weal, is victory!
We will not fight.

We will not fight!
We once were cowards; we could not resist
The lies of statesmen, cries of " Pacifist! "
But now we know that war is waged for gold —
And for men's profit shall our lives be sold?
We will not fight.

We will not fight!
You may imprison us in walls of stone —
Our souls, our consciences, are still our own.
We are not heroes, only sober men,
Who vow that war must never be again.
We will not fight.

Thomas Curtis Clark

The Old Men and the Young Men

Said the old men to the young men,
  ' Who will take arms to be free? '
Said the young men to the old men,
  ' We.'

Said the old men to the young men,
  ' It is finished. You may go.'
Said the young men to the old men,
  ' No.'

Said the old men to the young men,
  'What is there left to do?'
Said the young men to the old men,
  'You.'
Witter Bynner

Prayer for a World in Arms

O God of field and city,
  O Lord of shore and sea,
Behold us, in Thy pity,
  Lift naked hands to Thee.
Our swords and spears are shattered,
  Our walls of stone downthrust,
Our reeking altars scattered,
  And trodden in the dust.

O God of law unbroken,
  O Lord of justice done,
Thine awful word is spoken
  From sun to flaming sun —
We hate and we are hated,
  We slay, and lo, are slain,
We feed, and still unsated
  We hunt our prey again.

O God of mercy tender,
  O Lord of love most free,
Forgive, as we surrender
  Our wayward wills to Thee.
Absolve our fell allegiance
  To captain and to king;
Receive in full obedience
  The chastened hearts we bring.
John Haynes Holmes

In the Deep Caves of the Heart

In the deep caves of the heart, far down, running under the
    outward shows of the world and of people,
Running under continents, under the fields and the roots of
    the grasses and trees,
Under the little thoughts and dreams of men, and the history
    of races,
I see, feel and hear wondrous and divine things.
I seem to see the strands of affection and love, so tender, so
    true and life-long, holding together the present and past
    generations.
The currents of love and thought streaming in the watches
    of the night from far and near, from one to another,
Streaming all the more powerfully for the very hindrances
    and disasters which arrive or threaten.
I dream that these are the fibers and nerves of a body that
    lies within the outer body of society;
A network, an innumerable vast interlocked ramification,
    slowly being built up;
All dear lovers and friends, all families, groups, all peoples,
    nations, all times, all worlds perhaps,
Members of a body, archetypal, eterne, glorious, the center
    and perfection of life.
The organic growth of God Himself in time.

Edward Carpenter

From ' Towards Democracy '

The Price of Peace

Give up your mob-engendered thrills,
    Stuffed uniforms and braying trumpets
And warriors stepping high before
    Their sweethearts, wives, and leering strumpets.

Give up your crass hypocrisies;
  Your 'destiny' and 'white man's burden,'
Your twin rewards of bullying:
  The bandit's loot and hero's guerdon.

Give up your game of grab-and-keep,
  Your colonies, your naval bases,
Your insincere, self-warming cant
  Of 'noble' and 'ignoble' races.

Give up your smug moralities,
  Your heraldry, your star-and-garter,
'Protective' tariffs, much revered
  Diplomacy of wink and barter.

Give up your jungle politics,
  Your privilege, your double standard,
Your wrong-for-him-and-right-for-me,
  Your 'business interests,' pimped and pandered.

Go wash your hands and cleanse your heart
  And test your soul by zealous tasking:
Then bring your gifts and take the prize:
  It's yours, my Country, for the asking.

Homer C. House

In Flanders

Could you have seen them marching
  Ten thousand men in line,
You would have said that war must be
  Adventurous and fine.
You would have felt your pulses beat
  Fast to the tread of marching feet.

Could you have seen them marching
   Under the June blue skies
With all the glory of their youth
   Shining in their eyes,
You would have bade them all God speed
   To battle at their country's need.

But had you seen them creeping back
   In the grey, grey dawn,
The broken bleeding bodies
   With all their beauty gone,
Oh! never could you cheer again
   To see ten thousand fighting men.

James Norman Hall

The Lament of the Voiceless

' Wars are to be,' they say, they blindly say,
Nor strive to end them. Had we eyes to see
The ghosts that walk across the fields of slain,
We might behold by each boy soldier's corpse
An endless line who mourn his fateful doom.

' Who are you? ' asking, we might hear these words:
' We are the men and women not to be,
Because the father of our line was slain,
Cut off untimely. Brave he was and strong;
His heritage were ours had he not been
The food of slaughter in a wanton war.'

Boy soldier, sleep, by fireside loved ones mourned;
By neighbor comrades, half ashamed of life,
When death claims him who went that they might stay.

Boy soldier, sleep; if ever these forget,
You still are mourned by that long line unborn,
Who might have been but for the waste of war.
They mourn for you, your sons who never were.
Laura Bell Everett

The Prince of Peace

The Prince of Peace His banner spreads,
   His wayward folk to lead
From War's embattled hates and dreads,
   Its bulwarked ire and greed.
O marshal us, the sons of sires
   Who braved the cannon's roar,
To venture all that peace requires
   As they dared death for war.

Lead on, O Christ! That haunting song
   No centuries can dim,
Which long ago the heavenly throng
   Sang over Bethlehem.
Cast down our rancor, fear and pride,
   Exalt good will again!
Our worship doth Thy name deride,
   Bring we not peace to men.

Thy pardon, Lord, for war's dark shame,
   Its death-strewn, bloody fields!
Yet thanks to Thee for souls aflame
   Who dared with swords and shields!
O Christ, who died to give men life,
   Bring that victorious hour,
When man shall use for peace, not strife,
   His valor, skill, and power.

Cleanse all our hearts from our disgrace —
    We love not world, but clan!
Make clear our eyes to see our race
    One family of man.
Rend Thou our little temple veils
    That cloak the truth divine,
Until Thy mighty word prevails,
    That cries, ' All souls are mine.'

Harry Emerson Fosdick

Youth

We have heard the trumpets calling Youth,
We have seen their proud reply,
Laughing as they leapt to die,
Boyhood in their battle cry;
We have heard the world's tears falling
    For slain youth.

Still a sterner strife is calling Youth,
Madness beats upon the gates
Of old selfishness; age prates,
Cavils, queries, hesitates;
Nearer roars the storm, appalling
    All but Youth —

Youth that hears diviner voices, Youth
That has faith in brotherhood,
Courage to attempt a good
Only visioned yet, that would
Build a world where life rejoices,
    Generous Youth.

Katharine Lee Bates

A Hymn for the Pact of Peace

Lift up your heads, ye peoples,
  The miracle has come,
No longer are ye helpless,
  No longer are ye dumb.

Those whom ye craved to lead you,
  Your path of yearning dare,
The few rejoice with feasting,
  The millions praise with prayer.

Lift up your hearts, ye peoples,
  Cheer every doubting soul,
That found the road a barrier,
  Betwixt you and your goal.

Go say to him that feareth
  That peace is but a wraith,
'Not rulers but the people
  Shall seal the peoples' faith.'

Lift up your hands, ye peoples,
  And take the sacred vow,
'To war's age-honored Moloch,
  No longer will we bow.'

Your leaders who have followed,
  Arise and follow them,
Oh, hear ye not the angels
  Singing of Bethlehem!

Robert Underwood Johnson

The Arsenal at Springfield

This is the Arsenal. From floor to ceiling,
   Like a huge organ, rise the burnished arms;
But from their silent pipes no anthem pealing
   Startles the villages with strange alarms.

Ah! what a sound will rise — how wild and dreary —
   When the death-angel touches those swift keys!
What loud lament and dismal Miserere
   Will mingle with their awful symphonies!

I hear even now the infinite fierce chorus —
   The cries of agony, the endless groan,
Which, through the ages that have gone before us,
   In long reverberations reach our own.

On helm and harness rings the Saxon hammer,
   Through Cimbric forest roars the Norseman's song,
And loud, amid the universal clamor,
   O'er distant deserts sounds the Tartar gong.

I hear the Florentine, who from his palace
   Wheels out his battle-bell with dreadful din,
And Aztec priests upon their teocallis
   Beat the wild war-drums made of serpent skin;

The tumult of each sacked and burning village;
   The shout that every prayer for mercy drowns;
The soldiers' revels in the midst of pillage;
   The wail of famine in beleaguered towns;

The bursting shell, the gateway wrenched asunder,
    The rattling musketry, the clashing blade;
And ever and anon, in tones of thunder,
    The diapason of the cannonade.

Is it, O man, with such discordant noises,
    With such accursèd instruments as these,
Thou drownest Nature's sweet and kindly voices,
    And jarrest the celestial harmonies?

Were half the power that fills the world with terror,
    Were half the wealth bestowed on camps and courts,
Given to redeem the human mind from error,
    There were no need of arsenals and forts.

The warrior's name would be a name abhorrèd!
    And every nation, that should lift again
Its hand against a brother, on its forehead
    Would wear forevermore the curse of Cain!

Down the dark future, through long generations,
    The echoing sounds grow fainter and then cease;
And like a bell, with solemn, sweet vibrations,
    I hear once more the voice of Christ say, ' Peace! '

Peace! and no longer from its brazen portals
    The blast of war's great organ shakes the skies!
But beautiful as songs of the immortals,
    The holy melodies of Love arise.

Henry Wadsworth Longfellow

Brotherhood

There shall rise from this confused sound of voices
   A firmer faith than that our fathers knew,
A deep religion which alone rejoices
   In worship of the Infinitely True,
Not built on rite or portent, but a finer
And purer reverence for a Lord diviner.

There shall come from out this noise of strife and groaning
   A broader and a juster brotherhood,
A deep equality of aim, postponing
   All selfish seeking to the general good.
There shall come a time when each shall to another
Be as Christ would have him — brother unto brother.

There shall come a time when knowledge, wide extended,
   Seeks each man's pleasure in the general health,
And all shall hold irrevocably blended
   The individual and the commonwealth;
When man and woman in an equal union
Shall merge, and marriage be a true communion.

There shall come a time when brotherhood shows stronger
   Than the narrow bounds which now distract the world,
When the cannons roar and trumpets blare no longer,
   And the ironclad rusts, and battle flags are furled;
When the bars of creed and speech and race, which sever,
Shall be fused in one humanity forever.

Lewis Morris

Warrior Ghost

(To the dead on both sides)

We're sleeping now, my brothers,
   Beneath a battered sod,
Deep down in earth's rich bosom,
   A ransom to war's god.

I feel your pulse-beat, brothers,
   In dust below the grass —
Its whispering blades a-quiver
   As German breezes pass.

I spilled your blood, my brothers,
   Your knives tore through my breast,
But now I know you, brothers,
   We've gained a warrior's rest.

They call us dead, my brothers,
   (The weeds grow at our head)
Because we sleep together,
   At peace and comforted.

Don West

The Starred Mother

Is there a madness underneath the sun
More strange, more terrible? or any one
More pitiful than this, that for a star
A mother sells her flesh and blood to war?

A son for slaughter, and a star for praise!
Nor this the total madness of our days,
A son to slay some other mother's son,
And by such murder mother's blessing won!

The Hindu mother, by the Ganges tide
Drowning her babe, heart-broken, but with pride,
Poor blind purveyor to a Saurian feast,
Still spares her babe from murder's maw, at least.

Is there debauchery more deep than this?
The State betraying mothers with a kiss?
Bribing the Marys of the world to sell,
For tinseled star, their flesh and blood to hell!
Robert Whitaker

Peace

Peace in our time, O Lord,
To all the peoples — Peace!
Peace surely based upon Thy Will
And built in righteousness.
      Thy power alone can break
      The fetters that enchain
      The sorely-stricken soul of life,
      And make it live again.

Too long mistrust and fear
Have held our souls in thrall;
Sweep through the earth, keen breath of heaven,
And sound a nobler call!
      Come, as Thou didst of old,
      In love so great that men
      Shall cast aside all other gods
      And turn to Thee again!

O, shall we never learn
The truth all time has taught —
That without God as architect
Our building comes to naught?
>Lord, help us, and inspire
>Our hearts and lives, that we
>May build, with all Thy wondrous gifts,
>A Kingdom meet for Thee!

Peace in our time, O Lord,
To all the peoples — Peace!
Peace that shall build a glad new world,
And make for life's increase.
>O Living Christ, who still
>Dost all our burdens share,
>Come now and dwell within the hearts
>Of all men everywhere!

John Oxenham

Grass

Pile the bodies high at Austerlitz and Waterloo,
Shovel them under and let me work —
>I am the grass; I cover all.

And pile them high at Gettysburg,
And pile them high at Ypres and Verdun,
Shovel them under and let me work.
Two years, ten years, and passengers ask the conductor:
>What place is this?
>Where are we now?

>I am the grass.
>Let me work.

Carl Sandburg

A Carol for the New Year
(After the World War)

Blow, bugles, blow!
The dark days into old oblivion go.
Blow gladness from the summits of the world:
The battle-flags are furled —
Wild flags that startled up at every breath —
Banners that beat against the winds of death.
They have their rest at last,
Rich with heroic memories of the past.

Blow, bugles, blow!
The battle years have ended, and we go
Onward to meet the future with a song,
Knowing our might is greater than all wrong —
Knowing we have a key for every gate,
And that the heart has dare for every fate —
Knowing that God is in the years ahead,
As He was with us when the roads were red.

Blow, bugles, blow!
The shames and tyrannies begin to go.
Sing, bugles, sing into the ear of time
The end of the ancient crime —
Sing with a silver tongue,
Let all old faces gladden and grow young,
And let the hearts of youth
Sing with the glory of the world's New Truth —
The high glad brother-hail;
For nevermore must Love's great purpose fail —
Never again the hopes depart
Out of the world's joy-stilled, grief-greatened Heart.
Edwin Markham

A Voice Prophetic

Over the carnage rose prophetic a voice:
Be not disheartened — affection shall solve the problems of
 Freedom yet;
Those who love each other shall become invincible — they
 shall yet make Columbia victorious.
Sons of the Mother of All! you shall yet be victorious!
You shall yet laugh to scorn the attacks of the remainder of
 the earth,
No danger shall balk Columbia's lovers;
If need be, a thousand shall sternly immolate themselves for
 one. . . .
The dependence of Liberty shall be lovers,
The continuance of Equality shall be comrades,
These shall tie you and bind you stronger than hoops of iron.
Walt Whitman

Paradox

We are a regiment, whose martial cry
 Is the cry of peace! Above war's puppet dead
Our avenging banner trails across the sky,
 Till the sky itself streams red.

For each bewildered soldier flung to your foe,
 For every godlike man you force to a gun,
A comrade joins our army, to overthrow
 Your war till our war be won.

Trampling your law that kills, our steady tread
 Is matched by a ghostly echo: keeping our stride,
A brother walks with each from your enemy's dead,
 Your own slain march at our side.
Benjamin Musser

Good News

Let me be done for good and all with news
Of a mad world, proclaimed on every side
By orators who thunder and deride,
And bitter preachers shrieking: ' I accuse! '
And cynic quipsters scribbling to amuse —
Fierce wee colossi on mole-hills astride.
Where is the unreal world which they abuse?
What means the torrent of their wordy pride?

For there are folk in darkened city rooms,
Meek souls, in whom bright loving-kindness blooms;
And there are folk on lonely toilsome farms,
Kind souls, who live and die without alarms;
In them the eternal gospel speaks again,
And angels sing: Peace and good will to men.

Tertius van Dyke

Comrade, Remember

Comrade, within your tent of clay
   Waiting the march of ghostly legions,
The dead can speak. What do they say
   As they march to the heavenly regions?

Comrade, your peace is still and deep
   As God's own flesh burned to gray embers.
How can I honor you who sleep
   Where only God Himself remembers?

' Comrade,' he says, ' I am not dead,
   Nor is my last strange sentence spoken
As long as comrades mark the tread
   Of crippled feet and bodies broken.

'Remember them, and I shall die.
  Remember them and then, forgetting
Us dead, show them the clean white sky
  With the sun of peace never setting.'
Raymond Kresensky

The Land Where Hate Should Die

This is the land where hate should die —
  No feuds of faith, no spleen of race,
No darkly brooding fear should try
  Beneath our flag to find a place.
Lo! every people here has sent
  Its sons to answer freedom's call;
Their lifeblood is the strong cement
  That builds and binds the nation's wall.

This is the land where hate should die —
  Though dear to me my faith and shrine,
I serve my country well when I
  Respect beliefs that are not mine.
He little loves his land who'd cast
  Upon his neighbor's word a doubt,
Or cite the wrongs of ages past
  From present rights to bar him out.

This is the land where hate should die —
  This is the land where strife should cease,
Where foul, suspicious fear should fly
  Before our flag of light and peace.
Then let us purge from poisoned thought
  That service to the state we give,
And so be worthy as we ought
  Of this great land in which we live!
Denis A. McCarthy

Disarmament

'Put up the sword!' The voice of Christ once more
Speaks, in the pauses of the cannon's roar,
O'er fields of corn by fiery sickles reaped
And left dry ashes; over trenches heaped
With nameless dead; o'er cities starving slow
Under a rain of fire; through wards of woe
Down which a groaning diapason runs
From tortured brothers, husbands, lovers, sons
Of desolate women in their far-off homes,
Waiting to hear the step that never comes!
O men and brothers! let that voice be heard.
War fails, try peace; put up the useless sword!

Fear not the end. There is a story told
In Eastern tents, when autumn nights grow cold
And round the fire the Mongol shepherds sit
With grave responses listening unto it:

Once, on the errands of his mercy bent,
Buddha, the holy and benevolent,
Met a fell monster, huge and fierce of look,
Whose awful voice the hills and forests shook.
'O son of peace!' the giant cried, 'thy fate
Is sealed at last, and love shall yield to hate.'
The unarmed Buddha looking, with no trace
Of fear or anger, in the monster's face,
In pity said: 'Poor fiend, even thee I love.'
Lo! as he spake the sky-tall terror sank
To hand-breadth size; the huge abhorrence shrank
Into the form and fashion of a dove;
And where the thunder of its rage was heard,
Circling above him sweetly sang the bird:
'Hate hath no harm for love,' so ran the song;
'And peace unweaponed conquers every wrong.'

John Greenleaf Whittier

Christmas 1917

Is it a mocking jest that Christmas bells
   Chime in this tragic hour of strife and pain,
That in the misery of conflicting wills
   Breathless, men whisper words of love again?

Is it a jest that Europe's stainless snows
   In beauty mask her burning, bleeding scars,
Where man's blaspheming thunder comes and goes? —
   Is this unholiest his last of wars?

Is this the freedom that we bought so dear —
   To live among the wolf-pack in a cage,
Spurred by a Sycorax to hate and fear —
   Ingenious brutes that cower and kill and rage?

Have we no further end, no nobler plan,
   No subtler vision and no bolder will?
Is this the creature that we called a man?
   Is this the jungle that we live in still?

Be dumb! ye bells, nor wake the frosty air
   With joyful clamor while the nations bleed;
Let sorrow's silence speak a people's prayer
   Whose legioned sons lie crucified by greed.

Be dumb, sweet bells; or ring more wild and clear,
   Proclaim a sunrise on youth's Calvary!
Ring out the madness with the dying year,
   Let nations pass so Man himself be free.

Brent Dow Allinson

From The Terrible Meek

I am a soldier.
I have been building kingdoms for twenty years.
I have never known another trade.
Soldiery, brutality, bloody murder, that's my business.
My hands are crimson with it.
That's empire, that's what empire means.

In the city I come from,
It is the chief concern of the people.
Building kingdoms, building rule, building empires.
They're proud of it.
Little children in the schools are drilled
In obedience to it.
They are brought up to reverence its symbols.
When they wave its standard above them
They shout, they leap, they make wild and joyful noises,
Like little wolves, like little brute beasts.
Children, *young* children! And parents encourage them!
They never feel ashamed;
They would be treated like lepers if they felt ashamed!
That's what lust for empire does to folks.
It springs from a subtle fear,
A peculiar kind of fear that they call courage!

So we go on building our kingdoms,
The kingdoms of this world.
We stretch out our hands, greedy, grasping, tyrannical,
We stretch out our hands to possess the earth,
Domination, power, glory, money, merchandise, luxury,
These are the things we aim at;
But what we really get is pest and famine,
Grudged labor, the enslaved hate of men and women,
Ghosts, dead and death-breathing ghosts
That haunt our lives forever!

Already our kingdoms are beginning to totter.
Possess the earth?
Why, we have lost it! We never did possess it!
We have lost both the earth and our own souls
In trying to possess it!
For the soul of the earth is man and the love of man,
And of them both we have made a despair and a desolation!

I tell you, my good woman, this dead son of yours,
Disfigured, shamed, spat upon,
Has built a kingdom this day that shall never die.
The living glory of him will forever rule it.
The earth is his and he made it.
He and his brothers have been moulding and making it
Through all the long ages.

They are the only ones
Who ever really can possess it.
Not the proud, not the idle, not the wealthy,
Not the vaunted empires of this world. . . . No!
Something has happened here upon this hill today,
Something that will shake all the empires and kingdoms
Of this world into the dust.
The earth is his, the earth is theirs, and they made it.
The meek, the terrible meek,
The fierce, agonizing meek,
Are about to enter into their inheritance!
Charles Rann Kennedy

Call to Arms

Shoulder your guns and march away,
O brave young men, and don't ask why.
Give up your homes for soldiers' pay
And a treacherous life 'neath an unreal sky.

Forget what you've heard your fathers say
Of flaming woods, of men bleeding and raw;
Shoulder your arms and march away.
To kill is not always against the law.

The mighty of earth must snarl and spit
Over problems too deep for such as you;
Your part is to hurl yourselves into the pit
Where all of men's fears of hell come true.

You know quite well the reward for it:
A cross of honor, a tear, a spray
Of flowers, and prayers for your benefit . . .
Shoulder your guns and march away.

Helene Mullins

From The Poet in the Desert

O young men, with dawn behind your eyes
And Destiny held as a puzzling toy
Between your strong and nervous hands,
Why do you crowd forward to the sacrifice?
Young men who are about to die,
Stay a moment and take my hand,
Who am also about to die.
You have been carefully winnowed and selected
For the banqueting of the Hooded Skeleton
Which beckons, but says never a word;
I, too, would be satisfied
Why the young men must die,
And for what the maidens,
Treasure-caskets of the Infinite,
Must be robbed of the Gift
Preciously hoarded by the Miser Years.
Mystery — forever inscrutable.
Unanswered; unanswering.

Wonderful beyond wonder.
Two streams forever flowed red from two sides
Toward a dreadful brink
Where, through thick clouds,
Two crimson cataracts
Poured into everlasting Darkness.
Young men,
And even more than young men,
Young women,
Guardians of the Future,
Tell me distinctly for what is the sacrifice?
I demand that you refuse to be satisfied,
That you unravel the old shoutings,
That you peer to the very bottom.
Draw in your breath delightedly,
And confidently insist:
' My life is my Own.
' A gift from the Ages,
' And to me precious
' Beyond estimation.
' I will deny authority.
' I will question all things.
' I will obstinately be informed
' Whence comes the battle?
' Whose is the combat? '
Young men,
And even more than young men,
Young women,
I charge you that in the large solitude
Where the soul may meditate undisturbed,
And in the great crowds where souls jostle together,
Examine all things and refuse to be answered
Till you are answered of your own souls.

Charles Erskine Scott Wood

A Carol from Flanders

In Flanders on the Christmas morn
    The trenchéd foemen lay,
The German and the Briton born,
    And it was Christmas Day.

The red sun rose on fields accurst,
    The gray fog fled away;
But neither cared to fire the first,
    For it was Christmas Day!

They called from each to each across
    The hideous disarray,
For terrible has been their loss:
    ' Oh, this is Christmas Day! '

Their rifles all they set aside,
    One impulse to obey;
'Twas just the men on either side,
    Just men — and Christmas Day.

They dug the graves for all their dead
    And over them did pray:
And Englishmen and Germans said:
    ' How strange a Christmas Day! '

Between the trenches then they met,
    Shook hands, and e'en did play
At games on which their hearts were set
    On happy Christmas Day.

Not all the emperors and kings,
    Financiers and they
Who rule us could prevent these things —
    For it was Christmas Day.

O ye who read this truthful rime
From Flanders, kneel and say:
God speed the time when every day
Shall be as Christmas Day.

Frederick Niven

Cotton

That day when they spanned the cable from America to Europe they sang out gladly.
The cable, the huge ringing cable, set to work
and Europe said to America:
    Give me three million tons of cotton!
And three million tons of cotton roved over the sea
and changed to fabrics — fabrics with which one charmed
                            Senegambia's natives
and to gun-cotton — with which one killed them off.

    Sing aloud, sing aloud
    on all Senegambian trade routes!
      of cotton!
      of cotton!

Cotton, cotton, your white snowfall on the earth!
Your white peace be for our shrouds!
Your white, trailing robes when we wander into heaven
saved by Booth's jesus-face at all world ports!
    Cotton, cotton, your snowfall on the earth!
You fall like confetti of world events around the machines!

Translated by Llewellyn Jones from the Swedish of Harry Martinson. (From 'Modern Lyrik: en Antologi.' Bonnier: Stockholm. 1931)

Crucifixion

Golgotha's journey is an ancient way
    That leads from Rome's outrageous judgment gate
To modern slums and trenches, where we pray
    To Him whose heart is breaking with our hate.

We build His crosses now of steel and lead,
    And pierce His body with the bayonet;
Behind the trenches watch His blood flow red
    In flaming anguish that we soon forget.

Lord Caesar's high tribunal, Martian-wise,
    Spits in His face — Rome never was more rude! —
And in the name of freedom still denies
    To Christian men the right of rectitude.

For greed and self-enthronement are the same,
    And Jesus bleeds in every clan and clime;
All down the ages with its lashing shame
    He bears the insult — Love His only crime.

Hugh O. Isbell

Munition-Maker

' And in hell he lifted up his eyes, being in torment.'

Alone, from your dim cell you shall look forth; behold and see
Your perfect work! How faultless all your engines' butchery!
Your thirty pieces, what they bought in measure brimming o'er!
Those blackened fields; the shattered slain, where once was Spring before!
Silence — save where the blinded grope; a gasp from shredded lung —

A baby's wail; a crazy laugh the ghastly heaps among.
That vacant face that mouths at you; see, where the shambles stir —
The quick more dreadful than the dead! Your warplanes' lethal whirr —

Rejoice! was ever bargaining like this since time began?
And all for thirty bits! So well they paid you — every man
Whose flesh still writhes, or sleeps at peace; and does it sate your soul
To clutch your gold? Or would you blot from sight your monstrous toll?

Somewhere you too shall find the dawn. Somewhere you shall not miss
The joy of worlds no longer cursed by deeds the like of this.
Laura Simmons

Sadist Child

Young Mars threw out his brawny chest,
   Grabbed his helmet, hummed a tune,
Called for his tight-linked silver vest
   And hung his battle-axe on the moon.

' Oh, little earth,' the sadist said,
   ' Your restlessness has spoiled my sleep;
A million puny ant-men dead
   Will still your stirrings while you weep.'

And so an ugly rumbling thunder
   Told of the promise kept by Mars
Who, having righted earth's sad blunder,
   Returned to pluck the wings from stars!
Seymour Gordden Link

The Wounded Christ-Heart
(*Written in war-time*)

Anew He is wounded! The barbs of His wounding
   Are hurled by His Children — those marked with His name,
Who carry His banners, who ring forth hosannas —
   These robe Him with shame.

Anew He is wounded. The Temple He builded,
   The fabric He reared from the stream of His blood,
Is shivering with echoes that score Him, that shame Him,
   This Christ who built with His blood.

The Soul-of-the-world is aghast at its moorings —
   The rock of its faith that standeth secure —
It is racked by the breakers of sound that beat over
   Keen voices that follow the lure.

Oh the voices! These voices all barbéd that bruise Him!
   His own children's voices, once pledged and apart,
That shame Him — the Christ of the world-Soul immortal!
   They are wounding the Christ's loving heart.

George Klingle

Götterdämmerung

A god is dying, O bewildered ones,
   A greybeard god, whose zealous warriors
Have cowed the dismal world with bellowing guns
   Until the sky like some vast conch-shell roars.
A god is perishing from glut of praise
   From hypocrites whose tawny talons gleam
With secret gold which Judas-bright betrays
   Sad barter of their high birthright of dream.

Let trumpets burn with turbulence of morn
    While Jericho cracks down its house of glass.
A god is dying and a man is born;
    Let Mars and all his mangled mourners pass.
Here raise the sepulcher of creeds and kings
    Where peace, the Phoenix, lifts his golden wings!
Ernest Hartsock

Soldiers of the Light

God end War! but when brute War is ended,
Yet there shall be many a noble soldier,
Many a noble battle worth the winning,
Many a hopeless battle worth the losing.
      Life is battle,
Life is battle, even to the sunset.

Soldiers of the Light shall strive forever,
In the wards of pain, the ways of labor,
In the stony deserts of the city,
In the hives where greed has housed the helpless;
      Patient, valiant,
Fighting with the powers of death and darkness.

Make us mingle in that heavenly warfare;
Call us through the throats of all brave bugles
Blown on fields foregone by lips forgotten;
Nerve us with the courage of lost comrades,
      Gird us, lead us,
Thou, O Prince of Peace and God of Battles!
Helen Gray Cone

If War Should Come

Bar me in jail, where I can sing
   My song of love for erring man,
Flung by old men into this thing
   That never did and never can
Bring peace of God. My flag unfurled
Is of no country of this world.

For border-lines and nations are
   Less than one life, one heart that sees
A brother linked as star to star,
   Souls born for immortalities.
No wrong is righted in the will,
In peace or war, of those who kill.

Benjamin Musser

'No Quiet'

At last, 'All quiet on the western front';
No shrapnel singing fiercely as it came,
Intent to blight and mutilate and maim;
No big guns barking madly as their wont,
Upon their fiendish mission, born to stunt
The prey that crossed their path, small human game
Marked out for death, or fated to go lame,
Poor piteous trophies of the war-god's hunt.

All quiet? But a harshly mocking sound
Disturbs humanity's narcotic rest.
A host of voices shriek from out the ground,
'No quiet while you scoff at our behest,
While lust for war has held you gagged and bound,
While greed has charted and empowered your quest.'

Elinor Lennen

Wine for the King

What is the word of the wind? The word of the wind is
War! —
All of the olden horror! Moloch and Mars and Thor,
These supreme and sole, with Peace but a trampled thing,
Rapine and lust and famine, and blood for the wine of the
King!

Tears may gather and fall through all of the stricken lands;
The kine may brood in the stall, the harvest rot where it
stands;
The cup may be brimmed with gall, with the sweat of suf-
fering
For others — and yet, and yet, there must be wine for the
King!

What of the awful cost? What of the price to pay?
What of the loved and lost upon many a sanguine day?
What of the bells that toll? — Hark, how the echoes ring! —
Naught, for there must be wine — red, red wine for the king!
Clinton Scollard

The Bulwark of Liberty

What constitutes the bulwark of our own liberty and inde-
pendence?
It is not our frowning battlements, our bristling seacoast, our
army and our navy.
Our reliance is in the love of liberty which God has planted
in us.
Our defense is in the spirit which prizes liberty as the heri-
tage of all men in all lands everywhere.
Destroy this spirit, and we have planted the seeds of despo-
tism at our own doors.
Abraham Lincoln

The Flag Speaks

Brave men have followed
My irresistible
Beauty and magic:
Comradeship, loyalty,
High hearts' devotion
Shone in their faces
Fixed on my stars.

Tattered and blood-stained
In halls of honor,
I dream of my lovers
Whom I misled.

Cleansed of the blood-stain,
In the new morning
I call afar.

Not in one land alone,
Not in one tongue alone,
Not through one only flag,
Comes the new Word.

Leave the old death-dealing,
Leave the old fearing,
Lead on to life-giving —
Life, more abundant life —
Now it is day.

Never again in wars
Float my stripes, flash my stars:
I am the flag of life,
Sister of every flag
In the wide world.

Emily Greene Balch

The New Patriot

Who is the patriot? He who lights
  The torch of war from hill to hill?
Or he who kindles on the heights
  The beacon of a world's good will?

Who is the patriot? He who sends
  A boastful challenge o'er the sea?
Or he who sows the earth with friends,
  And reaps world-wide fraternity?

Who is the patriot? It is he
  Who knows no boundary, race, or creed,
Whose nation is humanity,
  Whose countrymen all souls that need;

Whose first allegiance is vowed
  To the fair land that gave him birth,
Yet serves among the doubting crowd
  The broader interests of the earth.

The soil that bred the pioneers
  He loves and guards, yet loves the more
That larger land without frontiers,
  Those wider seas without a shore.

Who is the patriot? Only he
  Whose business is the general good,
Whose keenest sword is sympathy,
  Whose dearest flag is brotherhood.

Frederic Lawrence Knowles

Make Way!

The crashing sky has swept old paths aside.
Old landmarks gone. Old bridges ground to dust.
The ferment, red with the defeating rust
Of spent illusions, bears no friendly guide.
No arrow of tradition points the turn.
In all the wilderness no voice calls ' Come! '
This is the desolation and the sum
Of all defeat. The ash spilled from the urn.

Yet, here in this black death, bitter to taste,
Out of the surging slime — a new design —
The substance fitted into better line
And form. The matrix purged of clogging waste.
Make way! Make way! From scourging pain shall rise
The flame that lights the candles in men's eyes.

Florence Crocker Comfort

No Armistice in Love's War

What are poets? Are they only drums commanding?
   Trumpets snarling, moving men to hate a ravage?
Were their songs of war the snares of Trade demanding
   Lives, and binding men to gods senile and savage?

What are soldiers? Only power, to be broken
   On the wheels of Business when there is no battle?
' War to end all war,' was that but falsely spoken?
   Whom has war set free? Have rifles stopped their rattle?

Many suffer hunger while the few still plunder.
   Dreams of peace and brotherhood are all undone.
Let poets' songs boom loud with love's own battle thunder!
   War has ended? No, the war has just begun.

Ralph Cheyney

The Song That Shall Atone

Ye shall hear of wars and rumors of wars: see that ye be not troubled.

Wild Europe, red with Wodin's dreadful dew,
On fire with Loki's hate, more savage than
Beasts that we shame by likening to man,
Was it toward this the toiling centuries grew?

Was it for this the Reign of Love began
In that young heretic, that gracious Jew,
Whose race his followers flout the ages through?
Is Time at last a mere comedian,

Mocking in cap and bells our pompous boast
Of progress? Nay, we will not bear it so.
A million hands launch ships to succor woe;
The stars that shudder o'er the slaughtering host

Rain blessing on the Red Cross groups that go
Careless of shrapnel, emulous for the post
Where foul diseases wreak their uttermost
Of horror. Saintship walks incognito

As scoffing Science, but Christ knows his own.
Sway as it may the war-god's fell caprice,
The victories of Love shall still increase
Until at last, from all this wail and moan,

Rises the song of brotherhood to cease
No more, no more — the song that shall atone
Even for this mad agony. The throne
That war is building is the throne of Peace.

Katharine Lee Bates

We Builders of Cities

We builders of cities and civilizations walled away from the
  sea and the sod
Must reach, dream-led, for our revelations through one an-
  other — as far as God.
Through one another, through one another, no more the
  gleam on sea and land,
But so close that we see the Brother, and understand, and
  understand!
Till, drawn in swept crowd closer, closer, we see the gleam in
  the human clod,
And clerk and foreman, peddler and grocer are one in the
  Family of God.

James Oppenheim

America Befriend

O Lord, our God, Thy mighty hand
  Hath made our country free;
From all her broad and happy land
  May worship rise to Thee.
Fulfill the promise of her youth,
  Her liberty defend;
By law and order, love and truth,
  America befriend!

The strength of every state increase
  In Union's golden chain;
Her thousand cities fill with peace,
  Her million fields with grain;
The virtues of her mingled blood
  In one new people blend;
By unity and brotherhood,
  America befriend!

O suffer not her feet to stray;
   But guide her untaught might,
That she may walk in peaceful day
   And lead the world in light.
Bring down the proud, lift up the poor,
   Unequal ways amend;
By justice, nation-wide and sure,
   America befriend!

Through all the waiting land proclaim
   The gospel of good will;
And may the joy of Jesus' name
   In every bosom thrill.
O'er hill and vale, from sea to sea,
   Thy holy reign extend;
By faith and hope and charity,
   America befriend!

Henry van Dyke

This is the Last

Coming in splendor through the golden gate
Of all the days, swift passing, one by one,
O silent planet, thou hast gazed upon
How many harvestings dispassionate?
Across the many-furrowed fields of Fate,
Wrapt in the mantle of oblivion,
The old, gray, wrinkled Husbandman has gone;
The blare of trumpets, rattle of the drum,
Disturb him not at all — he sees,
Between the hedges of the centuries,
A thousand phantom armies go and come,
While reason whispers as each marches past,
' This is the last of wars — this is the last! '

Gilbert Waterhouse

The Tournamant of Man

Clear the field for the grand tournament of the nations!
The struggle to think the best thought, and to express it, in tone and color and form and word;
The struggle to do the greatest deeds, and lead the noblest and most useful lives;
The struggle to see clearest and know truest and love strongest.
Your other blood and bludgeon contests but postpone the real fray.
The true knights are yearning to enter the lists, and you block the high festival with your brawling.
Is it possible you mistake this for the real event of history?
Away with your brutal disorder, and clear the field for the tournament of Man.

Ernest Crosby

Restoration

They look upon us through the mystic door,
Those who have passed, those who shall come to birth,
Waiting for us, the living, to restore
Beauty and fruitfulness to ravaged earth.
Where there were trees there must be trees again,
Sweet servants of the soil's imperious needs,
Because the Spring must not return in vain
Nor Autumn's bounty waste itself in weeds.
Where there was hope there must again be hope,
Undaunted beauty shining through the scars,
Because however men may fall and grope
They must not lose the everlasting stars.
It were the work of angels to revive
The orchard's fragrant ecstasy of flowers,
To bid the murdered forest wake alive —
The work of angels — and God makes it ours.

A still diviner labor to reflower
The spirit's orchards after hate's red blight,
And He, the Lord of Life, who understands
All things, has laid it in our faltering hands.
O Will of God, upon our hearts be power!
O Love of God, within our hearts be light.

Amelia Josephine Burr

On Syrian Hills

It is said the Bedouins cry on the Syrian hills a clear
Loud summons to war, and the tribes far distant hearken and hear,
So wondrous rare is the air, so crystal the atmosphere.
Their call is to arms; but One, in the centuries long ago,
Spake there for Peace, in tones that were marvelous sweet and low,
And the ages they hear Him yet, and His voice do the nations know.

Richard Burton

Love, Give Me the Feel of Tomorrow!

Come, love, help me move all the mirrors out of my workshop,
All the sore spots out of my heart!
You only can give me what I need:
A steel girder faith to build on,
The feel of tomorrow in my land.
Andante of a happy city's hundred thousand feet,
Keeping step in a grand procession,
Telling the world they walk in peace and freedom,
Broadcasting a forever-and-ever Armistice Day.

Ralph Cheyney

'Next Time'

The order goes; what if we rush ahead
   With friendly shouts — with welcoming and cheer
And loyal clasp of fellowship — instead
   Of lethal gas, and bombs that maim and sear —
              'Next time'?

If, in accord, the armies look afar
   Where droops a Figure on a Cross; and hear,
'Of all my woe, ye make a mockery!'
   With Him allied — what cause have we to fear —
              'Next time'?

Firm in our faith, we stand together there —
   Comrades and brothers; if we must be slain
So let our captains take us; but Beware!
   They cannot make us ope His wounds again —
              'Next time'!

Laura Simmons

A Song of Victory

But now above the thunder of the drums —
Where, brightening on, the face of Victory comes —
Hark to a mighty sound,
A cry out of the ground:
'Let there be no more battles: field and flood
Are weary of battle blood.
Even the patient stones
Are weary of shrieking shells and dying groans.
Lay the sad swords asleep:
They have their fearful memories to keep.
And fold the flags: they weary of battle days,
Weary of wild flights up the lonely ways.
Quiet the restless flags,
Grown strangely old upon the smoking crags.

Look where they startle and leap —
Look where they hollow and heap —
Now greatening into glory and now thinned,
Living and dying momently on the wind.
And bugles that have cried on sea and land
The silver blazon of their high command —
Bugles that held long parley with the sky,
Bugles that shattered the nights on battle walls —
Lay them to rest in dim memorial halls;
For they are weary of that curdling cry
That tells men how to die.
And cannons worn out with their work of hell —
The brief abrupt persuasion of the shell —
Let the shrewd spider lock them one by one,
With filmy cables glancing in the sun;
And let the blue-bird in their iron throats
Build his safe nest and spill his rippling notes.

' Let there be no more battles, men of earth:
The new age rises singing into birth! '
Edwin Markham

True Peace

Drums and battle-cries
Go out in music of the morning-star —
And soon we shall have thinkers in the place
Of fighters, each found able as a man
To strike electric influence through a race
Unstayed by city-wall and barbican.
Elizabeth Barrett Browning

From ' Casa Guidi Windows '

From Ad Patriam

                Land of my heart,
What future is before thee? Shall it be
To lie at ease, content with thy bright past,
Heedless of all the world, till idleness
Relax thy limbs, and swoln with wealth and pride
Shalt thou abandon justice and the poor?
Or shalt thou, re-awakened, scatter wide
The glorious tidings of a liberty
That lifts the latch of opportunity
First to thy children — then to all mankind?
Love of my soul — God keep thee strong and pure,
That thou shalt be a fitting messenger
To carry hope to all the sons of men.

William Dudley Foulke

The Internationalist

Though rains of jeering pelt with hissing sneers;
    Though winds of creeds their raucous bluster shout;
Though storms of sects and parties drench the land;
    Though gales of a derision howl about;

He stands in windy storming — stands alone,
    Whom sullen raining cannot pierce or soak;
For rooted in his faith, he calmly dons
    This darkened tempest like a warming cloak.

His brow is ploughed by bitterness of men,
    But scourges turn to tongues of glory yet!
His back is bent with folly of the world,
    Who takes his lashing for an epaulet!

Not all the anguish nor the bitter tears
    Can challenge Time as when his thought is heard;
Not all the thundering of all the guns
    Reverberates through ages as his word.

Banners of vision burn about his word:
    Destinies crowd and bow before his plan;
And Dawn, that kindles in his eyes, illumes
    The rising temple in the heart of man!
Louis Ginsberg

The Symphony

With instruments in ill-accord a hundred men
Thrum strings that hold sweet harmonies in leash,
Twisting the keys till practiced ears are satisfied:
    And then, enticingly, in cadences that surge
    And flow like billows on a granite shore,
    The genius of a Wagner casts a lingering spell.

These are not kinsmen, save as all mankind are kin;
Of birth and tongues diverse; of customs, creeds
And laws; of dear traditions. Bound by a single tie:
    And yet, entrancingly, in diapasons grand
    That first invite, then move, and then enthrall,
    The soul of some great master weaves a subtle spell.

The shadows of the crosses lie upon the fields.
The chastened peoples now have tuned again
Their instruments of peace. Waiting they thrum the strings:
    Now may there swell the strains majestic of a vast
    Symphony of will, sounding the war-lords' knell,
    As gently weaves the Master Soul his mystic spell.
Herman W. Stillman

Armistice

We face the nations with one hand outstretched
In greeting, and with peace upon our lips;
But in our hearts a question, in our minds
The haunting echoes of the song of war,
The song that sets the world a-tremble still
And shakes the very pillars of our faith.

How long before the peace can pass our lips,
Can claim our minds and drive out old distrust?
To doubt mankind is but to doubt ourselves.
When shall our fingers dare to drop the sword,
While with unquestioning eyes we reach two hands
In open comradeship to all the world?

Eunice Mitchell Lehmer

I Vow to Thee, My Country

I vow to thee, my country — all earthly things above —
Entire and whole and perfect, the service of my love,
The love that asks no questions: the love that stands the test,
That lays upon the altar the dearest and the best;
The love that never falters, the love that pays the price,
The love that makes undaunted the final sacrifice.

And there's another country, I've heard of long ago —
Most dear to them that love her, most great to them that know —
We may not count her armies: we may not see her king —
Her fortress is a faithful heart, her pride is suffering —
And soul by soul and silently her shining bounds increase,
And her ways are ways of gentleness and all her paths are peace.

Sir Cecil Spring-Rice

Locarno

The half-gods go; the centaurs, too.
The tarnished halos hang askew.
The startled hoof-beats, halted, hide
Upon a cross-scarred mountain-side,
Where trampled lovers all night through
Seek brides in wreaths of maiden's rue.
These, too, shall pass. A cooling dew
Has laid the ghosts of those who died —
    The half-gods go.

O seers, whose glow of vision blew
The haunted mists away, and you,
Unwedded elegists who cried
For gay young saviors crucified,
They rest beneath a dream come true:
    The half-gods go.

Earl Marlatt

The Path of Safety

The way to make war impossible is to be so strong as to make victory certain. — Mr. Winston Churchill

Two jolly German Barons lived in castles by the Rhine —
The noble Lord von Donnerblitz, the Graf von Schlagenstein:
Though truculent and haughty, they had been at peace for years,
For each was rather chary of the other's fifty spears:

Till the steward of von Donnerblitz observed to him one day,
'Through worry over Schlagenstein your hair is turning gray;

With this absurd equality of force one never knows
But what some little incident may see us changing blows.

' A learned man once told me, and I feel that he was right
" To the teeth you must be armed if you are anxious not to fight;
If you feel no taste for quarrels where the parties stab and hack,
You must be so strong that nobody can possibly attack."

' If another fifty lances you permit me to engage
You will never need to worry over neighbors in a rage,
In the peace of perfect safety we may cultivate the vine,
And you need not care a pfennig for the Graf von Schlagenstein.'

' Well said,' exclaimed his master, ' What a head the man has got!
Go forth, my faithful henchman, and enlist them on the spot.'
But this little conversation, by a traitor overheard,
Next morning to his rival was repeated, every word.

' Potztausend! ' quoth the latter, ' What the rascal says is true,
If you'd keep at peace with one, you must be strong enough for two;
So to put an end to panics, to suspicions, doubts and fears,
We'll increase at once our forces by a hundred lusty spears.'

On this, of course, his neighbor found a similar increase
Had imposed itself upon him — in the interests of peace:
So he hired some English archers at a most enormous salary
And re-fortified his castle with a machicoulis gallery.

Today each pays the wages of a thousand men-at-arms,
Yet neither knows a respite from suspicions and alarms;
And still two bankrupt barons are recruiting by the Rhine —
The noble Lord von Donnerblitz, the Graf von Schlagenstein.

Anonymous

From Locksley Hall

Men, my brothers, men the workers, ever reaping something new:
That which they have done but earnest of the things that they shall do:
For I dipt into the future, far as human eye could see,
Saw the Vision of the world, and all the wonder that would be;
Saw the heavens fill with commerce, argosies of magic sails,
Pilots of the purple twilight, dropping down with costly bales;
Heard the heavens fill with shouting, and there rain'd a ghastly dew
From the nations' airy navies grappling in the central blue;
Far along the world-wide whisper of the south-wind rushing warm,
With the standards of the peoples plunging through the thunder-storm;
Till the war-drum throbb'd no longer, and the battleflags were furl'd
In the Parliament of man, the Federation of the world.
There the common sense of most shall hold a fretful realm in awe,
And the kindly earth shall slumber, lapt in universal law.

Alfred Tennyson

Sew the Flags Together

Great wave of youth, ere you be spent
Sweep over every monument
Of caste, smash every high imperial wall
That stands against the new World State,
And overwhelm each ravening hate,
And heal and make blood-brothers of us all.
Nor let your clamor cease
Till ballots conquer guns.
Drum on for the world's peace
Till the Tory power is gone.
Envenomed lame old age
Is not our heritage,
But Springtime's vast release, and flaming dawn.

Peasants, rise in splendor
And your accounting render,
Ere the lords unnerve your hand!
Sew the flags together.
Do not tear them down.
Hurl the worlds together.
Dethrone the wallowing monster
And the clown,
Resolving only that shall grow
In Balkan furrow, Chinese row,
That blooms, and is perpetually young,
That only be held fine and dear
That brings heart-wisdom year by year
And puts this thrilling word upon the tongue:
'The United States of Europe, Asia and the World.'

'Youth will be served,' now let us cry.
Hurl the referendum.
Your fathers, five long years ago,
Resolved to strike, too late.

Now
Sun-crowned crowds
Innumerable,
Of boys and girls
Imperial,
With your patchwork flag of brotherhood
On high,
With every silk
In one flower-banner whirled —
Rise,
Citizens of one tremendous state,
The United States of Europe, Asia and the World.

The dawn is rose-dressed and impearled.
The guards of privilege are spent.
The blood-fed captains nod.
So Saxon, Slav, French, German,
Rise,
Yankee, Chinese, Japanese,
All the lands, all the seas,
With blazing rainbow flag unfurled,
Rise,
Rise,
Take the sick dragons by surprise.
Highly establish,
In the name of God,
The United States of Europe, Asia and the World.
Vachel Lindsay

The Valley of Decision

The World is in the Valley of Decision;
   It is standing at the parting of the ways;
Will it climb the steps of God to realm elysian —
   Or fall on horror of still darker days?

Will it free itself of every shameful shackle?
   Will it claim the glorious freedom of the brave?
Will it lose the soul of Life in this debacle,
   And sink into a mean dishonored grave?

All the world is in the Valley of Decision,
   And out of it there is but one sure road;
Eyes unsealed can still foresee the mighty vision
   Of a world in travail turning unto God.

All the world is in the Valley of Decision.
   Who shall dare its future destiny foretell?
Will it yield its soul unto the Heavenly Vision,
   Or sink despairing into its own hell?

John Oxenham

Over All the Lands

Over the prairies and over the mountains,
   And up from the cities that front the sea,
Out from the mills and the mines and the forests
   Is surging the call that shall set men free:

Refrain:
Over all the lands it sounds
   And over all the waters:
' Earth and the fruits of earth
   For all earth's sons and daughters!
No more each for each alone,
   But undivided,
   With hearts decided
We rise to claim our own! '

No more shall one man grow rich from another,
   Or greed of the few thwart the common good;
Children are we of the one Mighty Mother,
   As wide as the earth in our brotherhood.

Brothers shall build us the homes that we dwell in,
    And brothers shall till for our food the soil;
Brothers in freedom shall meet with each other,
    With gladness exchanging the fruits of toil.

Brothers shall sit in the council of peoples
    With old hates forgotten and war flags furled;
Brothers shall build us the ships and the railroads
    That bind us together across the world!
Anna Louise Strong

The Fatherland

Where is the true man's fatherland?
    Is it where he by chance is born?
    Doth not the yearning spirit scorn
In such scant borders to be spanned?
Oh, yes! his fatherland must be
As the blue heavens, wide and free!

Is it alone where freedom is?
    Where God is God and man is man?
    Doth he not claim a broader span
For the soul's love of home than this?
Oh, yes! his fatherland must be
As the blue heavens, wide and free!

Where'er a human heart doth wear
    Joy's myrtle-wreath or sorrow's gyves,
    Where'er a human spirit strives
After a life more true and fair,
There is the true man's birthplace grand,
His is a world-wide fatherland!
James Russell Lowell

A Mother Before a Soldier's Monument

Was it for this I braved a pathless, dark
   And chilling void, in travail while the hiss
   Of Death grew loud and near; from that abyss
To stumble back, enfolding in the arc
Of love-warm arms an infant life — a spark
   I fanned to ruddy glow? Was it for this
   I succored childish needs — healed with a kiss
Each wound that left, on flesh or pride, its mark?

Ah yes, for this I led my stalwart son
   In paths of rectitude; abhorring vice
   And choosing honor's way, he tossed the draft
That brimmed Youth's cup. . . . Bereft and old, I run
   Through War's red ledger — scan the costly price
   I paid for laurel wreath and marble shaft!
Winnie Lynch Rockett

Brotherhood

O Brother man! fold to thy heart thy brother;
   Where pity dwells, the peace of God is there;
To worship rightly is to love each other,
   Each smile a hymn, each kindly deed a prayer.

Follow with reverent steps the great example
   Of Him whose holy work was ' doing good ';
So shall the wide earth seem our Father's temple,
   Each loving life a psalm of gratitude.

Then shall all shackles fall; the stormy clangor
   Of wild war music o'er the earth shall cease;
Love shall tread out the baleful fire of anger,
   And in its ashes plant the tree of peace!
John Greenleaf Whittier

Architects of Dream

We cannot rest, whose hearts are like the breakers
   That pound forever in rebellious moan.
We cannot rest, who are the bright awakers,
   The trumpeters that mock the tyrants' throne.

We are the architects of dream, who cherish
   A beauty others never learned to feel.
The towers that we build shall never perish,
   For they are reared of spirit, not of steel.

We cannot rest, whose tongues are quick with pity
   For those who ply the ponderous wheel of toil,
The builders of the unsurrendering city
   To stand upon the new fraternal soil.

Lucia Trent

The New Loyalty

Let us no more be true to boasted race and clan,
But to our highest dream, the brotherhood of man.
Shall Babel walls of greed and selfishness divide?
Shall not the love of friends illume the patriot's pride?
For moated arsenals let shrines of art atone;
Where armies met in blood, let garden plots be sown.
Let royal hunting grounds be parceled out anew,
That little children's feet may know the grass and dew.

No more shall Mammon play with pawns of toiling men,
No more shall blood be spilled that Greed may count its gain.
Let patience be our power and sympathy our court,
With love our only law and faith our only fort.
New thoughts, new hopes, new dreams, new starry worlds to
   scan,
As Time proclaims the dawn, the brotherhood of man.

Thomas Curtis Clark

The Call of Brotherhood

Have you heard it, the dominant call
Of the city's great cry, and the thrall
And the throb and the pulse of its life,
And the touch and the stir of its strife,
As amid the dread dust and the din,
It wages its battle of sin?
Have you felt in the crowds of the street
The echo of mutinous feet
As they march to their final release,
As they struggle and strive without peace?
Marching why, marching where, and to what!
Oh! by all that there is, or is not,
We must march too and shoulder to shoulder.
If a frail sister slip, we must hold her,
If a brother be lost in the strain
Of the infinite pitfalls of pain,
We must love him and lift him again.
For we are the Guarded, the Shielded,
And yet we have wavered and yielded
To the sins that we could not resist.
By the right of the joys we have missed,
By the right of the deeds left undone,
By the right of our victories won,
Perchance we their burdens may bear
As brothers, with right to our share.
The baby who pulls at the breast
With its pitiful purpose to wrest
The milk that has dried in the vein,
That is sapped by life's fever and drain —
The turbulent prisoners of toil,
Whose faces are black with the soil
And scarred with the sins of the soul,
Who are paying the terrible toll

Of the way they have chosen to tread,
As they march on in truculent dread —
And the Old, and the Weary, who fall —
Oh! let us be one with them all!
By the infinite fear of our fears,
By the passionate pain of our tears,
Let us hold out our impotent hands,
Made strong by Jehovah's commands,
The God of the militant poor,
Who are stronger than we to endure,
Let us march in the front of the van
Of the Brotherhood valiant of Man!
Corinne Roosevelt Robinson

Pioneers

We shall not travel by the road we make:
   Ere day by day the sound of many feet
Is heard upon the stones that now we break,
   We shall be come to where the cross-roads meet.

For us the heat by day, the cold by night,
   The inch-slow progress, and the heavy load,
And death at last to close the long grim fight
   With man and beast and stone; for them the Road.

For them the shade of trees that now we plant,
   The safe, smooth journey and the final goal,
Yea, birthright in the land of covenant —
   For us day-labor, travail of the soul.

And yet the road is ours as never theirs!
   Is not one joy on us alone bestowed?
For us the Master-Joy, O Pioneers —
   We shall not travel, but we make the Road.
Author Unknown

How Shall We Honor Them?

How shall we honor them, our Deathless Dead?
With strew of laurel and the stately tread?
With blaze of banners brightening overhead?
Nay, not alone these cheaper praises bring:
They will not have this easy honoring.

How shall we honor them, our Deathless Dead?
How keep their mighty memories alive?
In him who feels their passion, they survive!
Flatter their souls with deeds, and all is said!
Edwin Markham

To One Who Denies the Possibility of a Permanent Peace

Old friend, I greet you! You are still the same:
You poisoned Socrates, you crucified
Christ, you have persecuted, mocked, denied,
Rejected God and cursed Him. In God's name
You monotonously threw to the flame
All those (whom now you honor) when the new
Truth stung their lips — for fear it might be true;
They reaped where they had sown, and felt no shame.
Familiar voice, old adversary — hail!
Yesterday's fools are now your gods. Behold!
The generations pass and we can wait.
You slandered even Florence Nightingale.
Now a new splendor quivers in the cold
Gray shadows overhead; *still* you are late.

Margaret Sackville

'Not to Destroy but to Fulfill'

While the proud garment of our common days
   Is spotted by this acid burn of wrong,
Though we would don it with averted gaze
   We may not walk unmindful of it long.
No thread of virtue that we deftly draw
   Across seared edges serves to hide the scar:
Defiled by murder in the name of law,
   The glass of truth reveals us as we are.

O Perfect Pattern, by the fair design
   That marked the beauty of Thy robe, we too
Would fashion ours with grace of fold and line
   Conforming to Thy stainless one!   Endue
Our eyes with vision to discern Thy will
   Who came 'Not to destroy but to fulfill.'
Molly Anderson Haley

For the New Age

The sound of anthems rarer grows and faint:
Shamed in his robes is many a mummering priest.
How empty now the sacerdotal feast —
Mere bread, mere wine, rises the vague complaint.
Now wider spread the canker and the taint
Of social woes by putrid creeds increased;
Loud grow the jeers of those once called the least
'Gainst pomp and panoply and crusted paint.

But underneath the tumult and the moan,
Beyond the jarring blows at Time's slow door,
God's groping orchestra cons o'er and o'er
That mightier music no man e'er has known.
Be calm, my soul, for soon the bell chimes clear
That all may know — the Better Days draw near!
Richard Warner Borst

Two Dwelling Places

For the finer spirits of (the world) there are two dwelling places: our earthly fatherland, and that other City of God.

Of the one we are the guests, of the other the builders.

To the one let us give our lives and our faithful hearts; but neither family, friend, nor fatherland has power over the spirit.

The spirit is the light.

It is our duty to lift it above tempests, and thrust aside the clouds which threaten to obscure it,

To build higher and stronger, dominating the injustice and hatred of nations, the walls of that city wherein the souls of the whole world may assemble.

Romaine Rolland

A Psalm of Confidence

The spirit of Man shall triumph and reign o'er all the earth.

The earth was made for Man, he is heir to all that therein is.

He is the end of creation, the purpose of the ages since the dawn of time.

He is the fulfillment of all prophecy and is himself the goal of every great hope born in high desire.

Who art Thou, O Spirit of Man?

Thou art the Child of the Infinite, in thy nostrils is the breath of God.

Thou didst come at Love's behest, yea! to fulfill the Love of the Eternal didst Thou come.

Yet Man's beginnings were in lowliness, in nature akin to that of the brute.

His body and appetite bore the marks of the beast, yet in his soul was the unquenchable Spark of Divine Fire.

His ascending hath been with pain, with struggle and conflict hath he marched towards the Ideal.

At times he hath turned his face away from the Promise of Destiny.

He hath given reins to the lust of the brute; he hath appeared at times as the Child of Hate.

He hath forgotten his Divine Origin, he hath forsaken the dream of Eternal Love.

Then hath he lifted his hands against his fellows and war and bloodshed have dwelt upon the earth.

In moments of blind passion he hath destroyed the work of his own hands, the fruit of the centuries hath he cast to the winds.

He hath marred the Divine Image, deaf to the call of the Promise of God.

Upon the altars of Self hath he sacrificed Brotherhood, and ruled by avarice and greed he hath slain Justice and Right.

Thus have wickedness and sin dwelt in his midst, and his soul hath been chained in the bondage of low desires.

Yet all this could not destroy the unquenchable Spark of Divine Fire.

For it belongs to the Eternal and that which is Eternal cannot die.

Therefore, great though Thy shortcomings, manifold though Thy failures, wicked though Thy crimes;

I will not despair, O Spirit of Man!

Thou canst not forever deny the God that is within Thee, nor turn Thy back upon the Ideal;

Though Thou destroyest fairest hopes yet shall they live again.

Though Thou returnest to the level of the beast Thou shalt arise to the heights of Thy Divine Humanity.

For the Spirit of Man breathes the untiring purpose of the Living God and to the fulfillment of that purpose the whole creation moves.

Stanton Coit

Prepare

O human hearts,
   Beating through fear, through jealousy,
   Through pride, through avarice, through bitterness,
Through agony, through death.
   Beating, beating,
   Shame and forgiveness,
   Bewilderment and love,
O my own country,
   My new world,
   Prepare,
   Prepare —
Not to avenge wrong
But to exalt right,
Not to display honor
But to prove humility,
Not to bring wrath
   But vision,
Not to win war
   But a people,
And not people only,
But all peoples,
Not to exact justice from your enemies only
   But from your friends,
And not from your friends only
   But from yourselves!

Witter Bynner

From The Mighty Hundred Years

It is the hour of man: new purposes,
   Broad-shouldered, press against the world's slow gate;
And voices from the vast eternities
   Still preach the soul's austere apostolate.

Always there will be vision for the heart,
  The press of endless passion: every goal
A traveler's tavern, whence we must depart
  On new divine adventures of the soul.
                              Edwin Markham

We Whom the Dead Have Not Forgiven

I cry to the mountains; I cry to the sea —
I cry to the forest to cover me
From the terror of the invisible throng

With marching feet the whole day long —
The whole night long.
Beating the accent of their wrong.

We whom the Dead have not forgiven
Must hear forever that ominous beat,
For the free, light, rippled air of heaven
Is burdened now with dead men's feet:

Feet that make solid the fluid space,
Feet that make weary the tireless wind,
Feet that leave grime on the moon's white face —
Black is the moon for us who have sinned.

And the mountains will not cover us,
Nor yet the forest nor the sea;
No storm of human restlessness
Can wake the tide or bend the tree.

Forever and ever until we die,
Through the once sweet air and the once blue sky
The thud of feet — the invisible throng,
Beating the accent of their wrong.
                              Sara Bard Field

The Greatest of These

A Paraphrase of I Corinthians, XIII

If I create wealth beyond the dream of past ages and increase not love, my heat is the flush of fever and my success will deal death.

Though I have foresight to locate the fountains of riches, and power to pre-empt them, and skill to tap them, and have no loving vision for humanity, I am blind.

Though I give of my profits to the poor and make princely endowments for those who toil for me, if I have no human fellowship of love with them, my life is barren and doomed.

Love is just and kind. Love is not greedy and covetous. Love exploits no one; it takes no unearned gain; it gives more than it gets. Love does not break down the lives of others to make wealth for itself; it makes wealth to build the life of all. Love seeks solidarity; it tolerates no divisions; it prefers equal work-mates; it shares its efficiency. Love enriches all men, educates all men, gladdens all men.

The values created by love never fail; but whether there are class privileges, they shall fail; whether there are millions gathered, they shall be scattered; and whether there are vested rights, they shall be abolished. For in the past strong men lorded it in ruthlessness and strove for their own power and pride, but when the perfect social order comes, the strong shall serve the common good. Before the sun of Christ brought in the dawn, men competed, and forced tribute from weakness, but when the full day shall come, they will work as mates in love, each for all and all for each. For now we see in the fog of selfishness, darkly, but then with social vision; now we see our fragmentary ends, but then we shall see the destinies of the race as God sees them. But now abideth honor, justice, and love; these three; and the greatest of these is love.

Walter Rauschenbusch

The Universal Republic

Upon the skyline glows i'the dark
The Sun that now is but a spark;
   But soon will be unfurled —

The glorious banner of us all,
The flag that rises ne'er to fall,
   Republic of the World!

Victor Hugo

Brotherhood

Your task is to form the universal family, to build the City of God, and by a continuous labor gradually to translate his work in humanity into fact.

When you love one another as brothers, and treat each other reciprocally as such; when each one, seeking his own good in the good of all, shall identify his own life with the life of all, his own interests with the interests of all, and shall be always ready to sacrifice himself for all the members of the common family — then most of the ills which weigh upon the human race will vanish, as thick mists gathered upon the horizon vanish at the rising of the sun.

Robert de Lamennais

From ' The Book of the People '

Build Me a House

Build me a House,
   Said God;
Not of cedar-wood or stone,
Where at some altar-place
Men for their sins atone.
To me, your only sin
Is to build my House too small:
Let there be no dome
To shut out the sky,
Let there be no cumbering wall.
Build me a House, a Home,
In the hearts of hungering men —
Hungering for the bread of hope,
Thirsting for faith, yearning for love,
In a world of grief and pain.
Build me a House!

Build me a World,
   Said God;
Not with a navy's strife,
Nor with a host in arms,
Compassing death, not life.
Build me a World, said God,
Out of man's fairest dreams;
Heaven must be its dome,
Lighted by prophet-gleams;
Justice shall be the stones
On which my World shall rise;
Truth and Love its arches,
Gripping my ageless skies.
Out of dreams, on the earthy sod,
Build me a World,
   Said God.

Thomas Curtis Clark

From Pioneers! O Pioneers!

Have the elder races halted?
Do they droop and end their lesson, wearied, over there beyond the seas?
We take up the task eternal, and the burden, and the lesson,
    Pioneers! O Pioneers!

All the past we leave behind;
We debouch upon a newer, mightier world, varied world;
Fresh and strong the world we seize, world of labor and the march,
    Pioneers! O Pioneers!

We detachments steady throwing,
Down the edges, through the passes, up the mountains steep,
Conquering, holding, daring, venturing, as we go, the unknown ways,
    Pioneers! O Pioneers!

See, my children, resolute children,
By those swarms upon our rear, we must never yield or falter,
Ages back in ghostly millions, frowning there behind us urging,
    Pioneers! O Pioneers!

On and on, the compact ranks,
With accessions ever waiting, with the places of the dead quickly filled,
Through the battle, through defeat, moving yet and never stopping,
    Pioneers! O Pioneers!

Oh, to die advancing on!
Are there some of us to droop and die? Has the hour come?
Then upon the march we fittest die, soon and sure the gap is filled,
    Pioneers! O Pioneers!

All the pulses of the world,
Falling in, they beat for us, with the western movement beat;
Holding single or together, steady moving, to the front, all for us,
    Pioneers! O Pioneers!

Has the night descended?
Was the road of late so toilsome? did we stop discouraged, nodding on our way?
Yet a passing hour I yield you, in your tracks to pause oblivious,
    Pioneers! O Pioneers!

Till with sound of trumpet,
Far, far off the daybreak call — hark! how loud and clear I hear it wind;
Swift! to the head of the army! — swift! spring to your places,
    Pioneers! O Pioneers!   *Walt Whitman*

Is It a Dream?

Is it a dream — and nothing more — this faith
That nerves our brains to thought — our hands to work
For that great day when wars shall cease, and men
Shall live as brothers in a unity
Of love — live in a world made splendid?

Is it a dream — this faith of ours — that pleads
And pulses in our hearts — and bids us look,
Through mists of tears and time, to that great day
When wars shall cease upon the earth, and men
As brothers bound by Love of Man and God,
Shall build a world as gloriously fair
As sunset skies, or mountains when they catch
The farewell kiss of evening on their heights?
    G. A. Studdert-Kennedy

INDEX OF TITLES

Ad Patriam (extract), *Foulke*, 60
America Befriend, *van Dyke*, 54
Architects of Dream, *Trent*, 71
Armistice, *Lehmer*, 62
Arsenal at Springfield, The, *Longfellow*, 26
Brotherhood, *Lamennais*, 81
Brotherhood, *Morris*, 28
Brotherhood, *Whittier*, 70
Build Me a House, *Clark*, 82
Bulwark of Liberty, The, *Lincoln*, 49
Call of Brotherhood, The, *Robinson*, 72
Call to Arms, *Mullins*, 39
Carol for the New Year, A, *Markham*, 32
Carol from Flanders, A, *Niven*, 42
Christmas, 1917, *Allinson*, 37
Comrade, Remember, *Kresensky*, 34
Confession of Faith, A, *Tolstoy*, 13
Cotton, *Martinson*, 43
Crucifixion, *Isbell*, 44
Cry of the Dead, *Ginsberg*, 10
Dawn, *Henderson*, 6
Desire of Nations, The, *Markham*, 3
Disarmament, *Whittier*, 36
Elegy for Mars, *Bostelmann*, 11
Fatherland, The, *Lowell*, 69
Flag Speaks, The, *Balch*, 50
For the New Age, *Borst*, 75
Gold Stars, *Cone*, 8
Good News, *van Dyke*, 34
Götterdämmerung, *Hartsock*, 46
Grass, *Sandburg*, 31
Greatest of These, The, *Rauschenbusch*, 80
How Shall We Honor Them? *Markham*, 74

Hymn of Hate, The, *Miller*, 10
Hymn for the Pact of Peace, A, *Johnson*, 25
I Vow to Thee, My Country, *Spring-Rice*, 62
If War Should Come, *Musser*, 48
In Flanders, *Hall*, 21
In the Deep Caves of the Heart, *Carpenter*, 20
Internationalist, The, *Ginsberg*, 60
Is It a Dream? *Studdert-Kennedy*, 84
Lament of the Voiceless, The, *Everett*, 22
Land Where Hate Should Die, The, *McCarthy*, 35
Locarno, *Marlatt*, 63
Locksley Hall (extract), *Tennyson*, 65
Love, Give Me the Feel of Tomorrow! *Cheyney*, 57
Make Way! *Comfort*, 52
Mighty Hundred Years, The (extract), *Markham*, 78
Mother Before a Soldier's Monument, A, *Rockett*, 70
Munition-Maker, *Simmons*, 44
New Earth, A, *Oxenham*, 16
New Loyalty, The, *Clark*, 71
New Mars, The, *Coates*, 15
New Patriot, The, *Knowles*, 51
'Next Time,' *Simmons*, 58
1914 — and After, *Oppenheim*, 13
No Armistice in Love's War, *Cheyney*, 52
'No Quiet,' *Lennen*, 48
'Not to Destroy but to Fulfill,' *Haley*, 75
Old Men and the Young Men, The, *Bynner*, 18
On Syrian Hills, *Burton*, 57

INDEX OF TITLES

Over All the Lands, *Strong*, 68
Paradox, *Musser*, 33
Path of Safety, The, *Anonymous*, 63
Peace, *Oxenham*, 30
Peace on Earth, *Freeman*, 9
Pioneers, *Author Unknown*, 73
Pioneers! O Pioneers! (extract), *Whitman*, 83
Poet in the Desert, The (extract), *Wood*, 40
Prayer for a World in Arms, *Holmes*, 19
Prepare, *Bynner*, 78
Price of Peace, The, *House*, 20
Prince of Peace, The, *Fosdick*, 23
Psalm of Confidence, A, *Coit*, 76
Restoration, *Burr*, 56
Sadist Child, *Link*, 45
Sew the Flags Together, *Lindsay*, 66
Soldiers, *Root*, 16
Soldiers of the Light, *Cone*, 47
Song of Victory, A, *Markham*, 58
Song That Shall Atone, The, *Bates*, 53
Starred Mother, The, *Whitaker*, 29
Symphony, The, *Stillman*, 61
Terrible Meek, The (extract), *Kennedy*, 38

This is the Last, *Waterhouse*, 55
To One Who Denies the Possibility of a Permanent Peace, *Sackville*, 74
Tournament of Man, The, *Crosby*, 56
True Peace, *Browning*, 59
Two Dwelling Places, *Rolland*, 76
Ultimatum, *Clark*, 18
Universal Republic, The, *Hugo*, 81
Valley of Decision, The, *Oxenham*, 67
Valley of the Shadow, The, *Galsworthy*, 14
Victory Without Peace, *Wood*, 7
Voice Prophetic, A, *Whitman*, 33
Warrior Ghost, *West*, 29
We Builders of Cities, *Oppenheim*, 54
We Whom the Dead Have Not Forgiven, *Field*, 79
Which Sword? *Pierce*, 17
Wild Weather, *Bates*, 12
Wine for the King, *Scollard*, 49
Wounded Christ-Heart, The, *Klingle*, 46
Youth, *Bates*, 24

INDEX OF AUTHORS

Allinson, Brent Dow
  Christmas, 1917, 37
Balch, Emily Greene
  The Flag Speaks, 50
Bates, Katharine Lee
  The Song That Shall Atone, 53
  Wild Weather, 12
  Youth, 24
Borst, Richard Warner
  For the New Age, 75
Bostelmann, Carl John
  Elegy for Mars, 11
Browning, Elizabeth Barrett
  True Peace, 59
Burr, Amelia Josephine
  Restoration, 56
Burton, Richard
  On Syrian Hills, 57
Bynner, Witter
  Prepare, 78
  The Old Men and the Young Men, 18
Carpenter, Edward
  In the Deep Caves of the Heart, 20
Cheyney, Ralph
  Love Give Me the Feel of Tomorrow! 57
  No Armistice in Love's War, 52
Clark, Thomas Curtis
  Build Me a House, 82
  The New Loyalty, 71
  Ultimatum, 18
Coates, Florence Earle
  The New Mars, 15
Coit, Stanton
  A Psalm of Confidence, 76
Comfort, Florence Crocker
  Make Way! 52
Cone, Helen Gray
  Gold Stars, 8
  Soldiers of the Light, 47

Crosby, Ernest
  The Tournament of Man, 56
Everett, Laura Bell
  The Lament of the Voiceless, 22
Field, Sara Bard
  We Whom the Dead Have Not Forgiven, 79
Fosdick, Harry Emerson
  The Prince of Peace, 23
Foulke, William Dudley
  Ad Patriam (extract), 60
Freeman, Robert
  Peace on Earth, 9
Galsworthy, John
  The Valley of the Shadow, 14
Ginsberg, Louis
  Cry of the Dead, 10
  The Internationalist, 60
Haley, Molly Anderson
  'Not to Destroy but to Fulfill,' 75
Hall, James Norman
  In Flanders, 21
Hartsock, Ernest
  Götterdämmerung, 46
Henderson, Daniel
  Dawn, 6
Holmes, John Haynes
  Prayer for a World in Arms, 19
House, Homer C.
  The Price of Peace, 20
Hugo, Victor
  The Universal Republic, 81
Isbell, Hugh O.
  Crucifixion, 44
Johnson, Robert Underwood
  A Hymn for the Pact of Peace, 25
Kennedy, Charles Rann
  The Terrible Meek (extract), 38

INDEX OF AUTHORS

Klingle, George
  The Wounded Christ-Heart, 46
Knowles, Frederic Lawrence
  The New Patriot, 51
Kresensky, Raymond
  Comrade, Remember, 34
Lamennais, Robert de
  Brotherhood, 81
Lehmer, Eunice Mitchell
  Armistice, 62
Lennen, Elinor
  'No Quiet,' 48
Lincoln, Abraham
  The Bulwark of Liberty, 49
Lindsay, Vachel
  Sew the Flags Together, 66
Link, Seymour Gordden
  Sadist Child, 45
Longfellow, Henry Wadsworth
  The Arsenal at Springfield, 26
Lowell, James Russell
  The Fatherland, 69
Markham, Edwin
  A Carol for the New Year, 32
  A Song of Victory, 58
  How Shall We Honor Them? 74
  The Desire of Nations, 3
  The Mighty Hundred Years (extract), 78
Marlatt, Earl
  Locarno, 63
Martinson, Harry
  Cotton (trans. by Llewellyn Jones), 43
McCarthy, Denis A.
  The Land Where Hate Should Die, 35
Miller, Joseph Dana
  The Hymn of Hate, 10
Morris, Lewis
  Brotherhood, 28
Mullins, Helene
  Call to Arms, 39
Musser, Benjamin
  If War Should Come, 48
  Paradox, 33
Niven, Frederick
  A Carol from Flanders, 42

Oppenheim, James
  1914 — and After, 13
  We Builders of Cities, 54
Oxenham, John
  A New Earth, 16
  Peace, 30
  The Valley of Decision, 67
Pierce, Jason Noble
  Which Sword? 17
Rauschenbusch, Walter
  The Greatest of These, 80
Robinson, Corinne Roosevelt
  The Call of Brotherhood, 72
Rockett, Winnie Lynch
  A Mother Before a Soldier's Monument, 70
Rolland, Romaine
  Two Dwelling Places, 76
Root, Merrill
  Soldiers, 16
Sackville, Margaret
  To One Who Denies the Possibility of a Permanent Peace, 74
Sandburg, Carl
  Grass, 31
Scollard, Clinton
  Wine for the King, 49
Simmons, Laura
  Munition-Maker, 44
  'Next Time,' 58
Spring-Rice, Sir Cecil
  I Vow to Thee, My Country, 62
Stillman, Herman W.
  The Symphony, 61
Strong, Anna Louise
  Over All the Lands, 68
Studdert-Kennedy, G. A.
  Is It a Dream? 84
Tennyson, Alfred
  Locksley Hall (extract), 65
Tolstoy, Leo
  A Confession of Faith, 13
Trent, Lucia
  Architects of Dream, 71
van Dyke, Henry
  America Befriend, 54

INDEX OF AUTHORS

van Dyke, Tertius
  Good News, 34
Waterhouse, Gilbert
  This is the Last, 55
West, Don
  Warrior Ghost, 29
Whitaker, Robert
  The Starred Mother, 29
Whitman, Walt
  A Voice Prophetic, 33

  Pioneers, O Pioneers (extract), 83
Whittier, John Greenleaf
  Brotherhood, 70
  Disarmament, 36
Wood, Charles Erskine Scott
  The Poet in the Desert (extract), 40
Wood, Clement
  Victory Without Peace, 7

ACKNOWLEDGMENTS

To both poets and publishers, sincere thanks and appreciation are given for their generous coöperation in permitting the use of the poems included in this anthology. Special acknowledgment is made to the following publishers, who have granted permission for the reprinting of copyrighted poems indicated:

The Macmillan Company for the use of *Sew the Flags Together*, by Vachel Lindsay, from his 'Collected Poems,' and the poem by Alfred Tennyson.

Charles Scribner's Sons: for *America Befriend*, by Henry van Dyke, *The Valley of the Shadow*, by John Galsworthy, and *The Call of Brotherhood*, by Corinne Roosevelt Robinson.

Bobbs-Merrill Company: for *On Syrian Hills*, by Richard Burton, from his 'Collected Poems.'

The Pilgrim Press: for *The Greatest of These*, by Walter Rauschenbusch, from his volume, 'Prayers of the Social Awakening.'

Henry Holt & Company: for *Grass*, by Carl Sandburg, from his volume 'Cornhuskers.'

Houghton Mifflin Company: for *Wine for the King*, by Clinton Scollard, from his volume 'The Singing Heart,' and for the poems of Whittier and Longfellow.

Harper & Brothers: for the extract from *The Terrible Meek*, from the volume under that title.

Alfred A. Knopf: for *Prepare*, by Witter Bynner, from 'A Canticle of Pan,' and *The Old Men and the Young Men*, also by Mr. Bynner, from 'Caravan.'

The Vanguard Press: for the extract from *The Poet in the Desert*, by Charles Erskine Scott Wood, from the volume under that title.

William Rudge: for *We Whom the Dead Have Not Forgiven*, by Sara Bard Field, from 'The Pale Woman.'

Thanks are due also to The Christian Century and World Affairs,

ACKNOWLEDGMENTS

which magazines generously granted permission to reprint poems originally published in their columns.

Acknowledgment is also made to Mrs. George S. Burgess, who granted permission to include the three poems of Katharine Lee Bates; to Benjamin Musser, for the use of his poem *If War Should Come,* reprinted from the magazine, Driftwood; to Mrs. Denis A. McCarthy, for the use of *The Land Where Hate Should Die,* by Denis A. McCarthy, from the volume under that title; to Edwin Markham, for the use of his five poems, from his 'Collected Poems' now in preparation (these poems are copyrighted by Mr. Markham and are used with his special permission); to John Oxenham, John Haynes Holmes, Robert Underwood Johnson, Charles Rann Kennedy, Witter Bynner, Charles Erskine Scott Wood, Sara Bard Field, Homer C. House, Laura Simmons, Richard Burton, Lucia Trent and Ralph Cheyney, who gave personal permission to reprint their poems; also to Henry Harrison, for permission to use Benjamin Musser's *Paradox,* and to Mrs. Jessie Rittenhouse Scollard, who added her permission for the reprinting of Clinton Scollard's *Wine for the King.*

Should there be any question regarding the use of any poem, regret is here acknowledged for such error. The compilers will be pleased, upon notification of such oversight, to make proper acknowledgment in future editions of this book.

THE COMPILERS